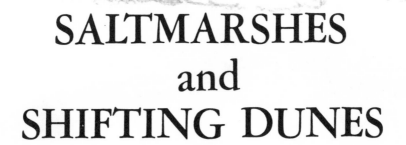

SALTMARSHES
and
SHIFTING DUNES

by JOHN F. WATERS

Illustrated by HARIS PETIE

HARVEY HOUSE, INC.
Publishers
Irvington-on-Hudson, N.Y. 10533

Manufactured in the United States of America
Library of Congress Catalog Card No.: 72-89779

HARVEY HOUSE, INC.
Publishers
Irvington-on-Hudson, N.Y. 10533

6

A tiny spit of land composed of sand and grass, mud and water, lies along the coast of Cape Cod, Massachusetts. On one side of the land is a saltmarsh, which is part sea and part land.

This marshy lowland is always damp, because the sea rises and covers the land during the floodtides of the new and the full moons. It is also spongy, because underneath the marsh grass is a layer of partially decayed vegetable matter, called peat.

Here, in this marshy land, birds, sea animals, mammals, and many other small creatures abound. Here, also, in the quiet early morning hours a tall, blue heron may often be seen poised on one leg, patiently waiting to gulp a fish down its long, thin neck.

A variety of plants, some of which burst into yellow, pink, and red flowers in the spring, grow along the edges of the saltmarsh.

7

Along this coast the shifting sand dunes tower above the marsh and overlook the sea. Their slopes are smooth and are covered at the top with tousled beach grass. At their base the sand spreads out to form a beach that stretches down to and beyond the edge of the water. As the waves rise and then fall, they crash into foamy bubbles that spread across the sand.

Scattered along this shore large, seaweed-covered rocks rise, hiding scores of salt-water pools that have been carved out of the rocks by the breaking waves. Some sea animals live in these pools, but the birds and the mammals inhabit the beach because they prefer drier surroundings. Flocks of tiny sandpipers scamper along the edge of the sea searching for bits of food. As each wave approaches, they wiggle their brown and gray bodies and "skitter" up the beach to stay out of reach of the flowing sea. When the tide ebbs, the sandpipers turn their tiny bodies quickly and skim along to the edge of the water.

Farther up the beach many plants that need a minimum of fresh water in order to thrive, spread their roots along the arid land.

Therein lies the difference between saltmarshes and shifting dunes. The marsh land is almost always wet, and the dunes and the upper part of the beach are almost always dry.

The Saltmarsh

To the east, beyond the sand dune, flows a salt-water tidal creek.
As the tide rises, the creek fills. When the tide ebbs, the creek
empties, leaving behind it little pools, wide, shallow streams, and
narrow, muddy beaches. In the streams tiny shrimp dart in and out,
hiding under the overhanging clumps of peat that form the banks
of the creek. On the bottom of one stream may be seen a hermit
crab peering out from its borrowed shell. This crab uses its two
large claws to rip and tear at anything that seems as if it might be
good to eat. As the crab crawls along, it drags the shell behind it,
and when it outgrows that shell or loses it, it searches for a larger one.
If it finds one, it makes sure that the shell is empty, and then it slips inside. When two hermit crabs want the same shell, there is a savage
fight until one of them gives up. The loser then crawls away to
continue its hunt for a shell, covering its soft body in the rear with
bits of seaweed or other debris as if it were ashamed of being seen.

As the water in the tidal creek rises, a black duck paddles slowly, using its bright red feet to push itself forward. It nibbles at the plants it finds, while its mate sits on the nest on higher ground and preens her feathers with her yellow bill. Underneath her downy body are nine, light-tan eggs. Suddenly she snaps her head around as something frightens her. Fear glares in her eyes. But she soon realizes there is no need to be alarmed, as it is only a harmless horseshoe crab plowing along the creek bottom.

This strange creature is not really a crab, but is related to the scorpion and the spider. Sometimes it is called the "king crab." It has five pairs of walking legs: The four front pairs are used for lifting, and the powerful back pair are used to drive the crab forward.

During the spring floodtides along the marshes, horseshoe crabs mate in peculiar fashion, the male attaching himself to the rear of the much larger female crab. They then cruise together through the shallow water, the female looking for a soft area in which to lay her eggs. She often scratches a hole in the soft sand and deposits as many as 200 eggs about the size of an "o." In a month, when the roses are in full bloom, tiny, tailless horseshoe crabs, one-quarter inch in length, appear and begin to swim upside down in the tidal creek, leaving their birthplace far behind. During the summer and fall, the outside covering of the crab will often split horizontally along the front, and out of it will crawl that same crab, now a bit larger, since it has outgrown its present hard shell. Within a year the bulldozer-like crab will be more than an inch in length, and when full grown, it will become at least two feet long.

Early settlers gave the horseshoe crab its name, since it resembles the shape of a horse's hoof. Sometimes the shell is divided into four quarters and is used by lobstermen as lobster bait. If a whole shell is found, it makes a fine bucket to bail the water out of a rowboat.

Marine scientists call the horseshoe crab a living fossil, since it has remained in existence on earth with little change for over 300 million years.

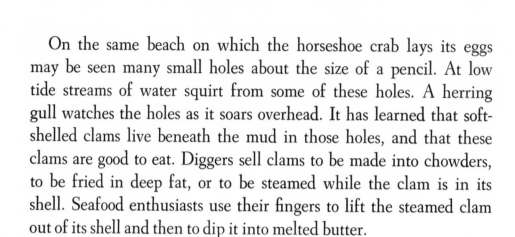

On the same beach on which the horseshoe crab lays its eggs may be seen many small holes about the size of a pencil. At low tide streams of water squirt from some of these holes. A herring gull watches the holes as it soars overhead. It has learned that soft-shelled clams live beneath the mud in those holes, and that these clams are good to eat. Diggers sell clams to be made into chowders, to be fried in deep fat, or to be steamed while the clam is in its shell. Seafood enthusiasts use their fingers to lift the steamed clam out of its shell and then to dip it into melted butter.

The sea gull has its own special way of preparing clams. It snatches one up in its beak, flies over a rock or a lonely coastal road and drops the clam, breaking the shell to pieces. Then it swoops down, picks the shell apart, and gobbles down the raw clam.

Many sea gulls are beach scavengers and will eat almost anything, even dead crabs or orange peels that have been washed up on the beach. The herring, the most common of the gulls, has likewise learned the trick of diving into shallow water to catch small minnows. This gull is a handsome bird, with a pure white body and grayish-blue wings tipped in black.

In the shallow streams a horseshoe crab may plow through the mud to uncover a small, hard-shell clam, called a quahog. Sea gulls also drop these on rocks to break the shell and then eat the raw clam. People also eat raw clams, calling them "little necks" and "cherrystones." The meat of a large quahog, a "bull" or a "coconut," as fishermen call these clams, also makes a good chowder.

Years and years ago, the Indians waded barefooted along the coast of Massachusetts and "squished" the mud with their toes until they found the quahog. The meat tasted good, and they used the shell for wampum, the Indian form of money. The inner, pearl-like shell, with its many tints of blue and silver, has been used for years to make mother-of-pearl buttons.

The shallow water in the saltmarshes has another strange inhabitant. This is the scallop. Two ruffled shells open slowly, then snap shut, causing the animal to zigzag about, squirting water crazily in every direction. The scallop's odd motion is due to a huge muscle, which closes the shells and sends out jets of water from either side of the hinge.

In the fall, shell fishermen collect the scallops, using wooden boxes open at the top and with a glass bottom. Clad in black rubber hip boots, the fishermen walk through the shallow water and place the box on the surface of the water. They can then peer through the glass bottom as they search for the scallop. The glass cuts down the glare of the sun on the water, and the fishermen are thus able to see the bottom more clearly. After they have collected the scallops, they pry them open, cut out the chunky, white muscle, wash it, and then fry it in deep fat.

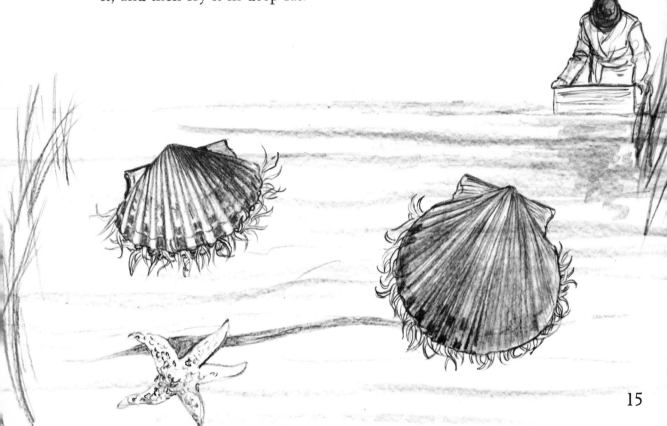

15

Living also in the mud in shallow water is the clamworm. This red and purple worm has many pairs of paddles which it uses for breathing and swimming. It hides in its underwater burrow during the day in a long, slanted hole in the mud or sand. At night it creeps out, a bit at a time, checking every square inch around its burrow and constantly on the alert for danger. Horseshoe crabs, fish, and other marine animals find the clamworm desirable as food. If the worm senses the slightest disturbance, it shrinks back into its burrow until the danger has passed. Boys who live near the sea dig up the clamworm and use it for bait when they go fishing, placing it on the end of the hook and lowering it into the water.

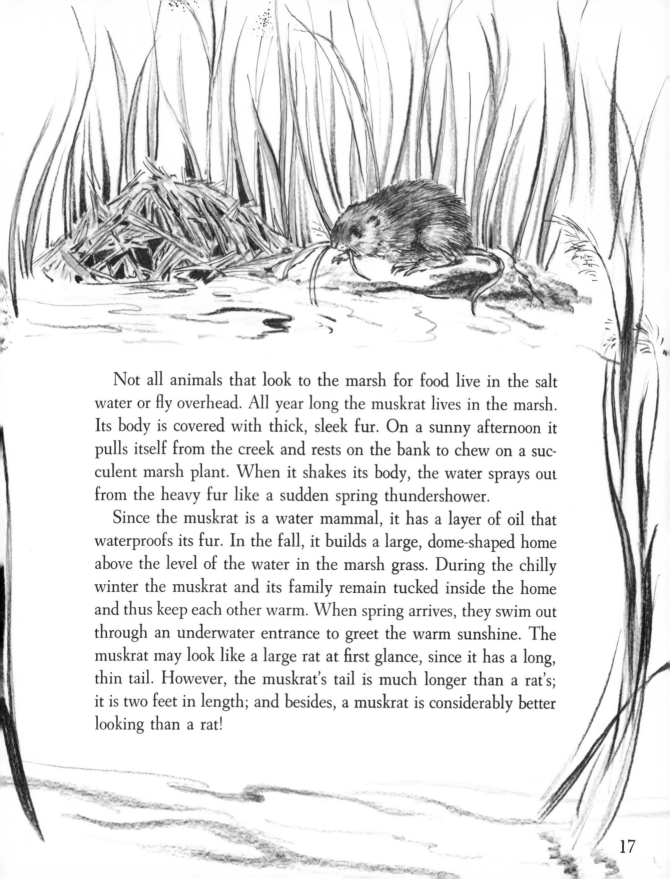

Not all animals that look to the marsh for food live in the salt water or fly overhead. All year long the muskrat lives in the marsh. Its body is covered with thick, sleek fur. On a sunny afternoon it pulls itself from the creek and rests on the bank to chew on a succulent marsh plant. When it shakes its body, the water sprays out from the heavy fur like a sudden spring thundershower.

Since the muskrat is a water mammal, it has a layer of oil that waterproofs its fur. In the fall, it builds a large, dome-shaped home above the level of the water in the marsh grass. During the chilly winter the muskrat and its family remain tucked inside the home and thus keep each other warm. When spring arrives, they swim out through an underwater entrance to greet the warm sunshine. The muskrat may look like a large rat at first glance, since it has a long, thin tail. However, the muskrat's tail is much longer than a rat's; it is two feet in length; and besides, a muskrat is considerably better looking than a rat!

At low tide a curious little animal runs in and out of a hole on the muddy marsh beach at the line where the mud and the sand mix, and where the marsh grass begins to grow. The male animal has one claw that is larger than the other. It holds this claw horizontally as it runs out of the hole, grasping a ball of sand which it deposits near the entrance. Then it scurries back inside, and a few seconds later, it comes out with another ball of sand. This strange-looking marine animal is called the "fiddler crab" since it holds its large claw in a way similar to the manner in which a fiddler holds his violin. The fiddler crab has eight legs, two claws, and two eyes that stick straight up on stalks as though they were tied to the ends of a pair of stilts.

Although the fiddler crab has no ears, it is able to tell that other animals are near when it "feels" slight movement of footsteps on the marsh floor. If it is disturbed by vibrations, the fiddler crab scoots inside its burrow until the vibration has ceased. This crab lives in the marsh with hundreds of its neighbors, all of them darting in and out of the grasses to feed on bits of plants found in the mud. It is difficult for a person to sneak up to look at them, since any sudden movement will cause the fiddlers to disappear. All that will be seen will be hundreds of mysterious holes with mounds of sand piled neatly on the outside.

A fiddler crab can move sideways, frontwards, or backwards, and when it runs, it uses only three of its eight legs. One of the larger crabs, the green crab, lives within the banks of the tidal creek and makes openings about the size of a fist in the bank. These tunnels extend to many little caves in the soft peat, but each tunnel always leads to another opening which the crab can use for an escape route.

Many tiny marine animals are collected alive to be studied in laboratories. One of these animals, the scallop, has several blue eyes along the inside edge of its shell. Since these eyes are very simple in structure, scientists, called marine biologists, examine the eyes of the scallop. Scientists have also studied the eyes of the adult horseshoe crab, and what they have learned from these experiments can be related to the human eye. With this information, medical men are able to perform eye operations with greater skill and to cure certain diseases of the eye.

The quahog has a substance that has been found to be useful in the fight against cancer. The fiddler crab, it has been discovered, has an inner biological clock that tells it when the tides are high and when they are low, even though the crab may be in a dark room where it cannot see the ocean or even the sun. Scientists believe that man also has a biological clock. When people travel long distances over oceans and across continents, they should plan to leave a day or two early in order to adjust themselves to a new time schedule. Today, researchists in many laboratories located in the scientific centers of the world continue to find new answers to old and new problems from the animals of the sea and the marsh.

The marsh is one of the most interesting in all the realm of nature. The tall, thin marsh grass, which is light green in spring, deep green in summer, and golden brown in fall, turns the marsh into one of the most beautiful areas by the sea, regardless of the season of the year. During the summer the cattails in the marsh grow tall, and the marsh winds brush them into a sea of flowing, dark green waves. Colorful birds, such as the red-winged blackbird, build nests in May or June throughout the marsh. The blackbird is a striking beauty; it is mostly black but has bright red shoulder patches. When the male and the female mate, they hide their nest among the tall grasses. If anyone should come too close to the nest, both birds screech to warn those who would dare to disturb them.

There are many larger birds that visit the marsh. During the early evening, when the sky is red with the setting sun, eight Canadian geese, mother, father, and six goslings, may paddle up the tidal creek to search for plants. Sometimes a boy and a girl will stand by the edge of the creek, bags of cracked corn in their hands. When the gander notices the corn, he will lead his family in a long line toward the bank. These geese have been fed so often by boys and girls that they show little fear. The six goslings begin at once to peck at the corn, squishing the salt water out of the rear of their bills. The mother goose also begins to eat, while the father goose stands his watch. He is not afraid, but he is cautious. When the mother has eaten enough, she raises her head, and the father goose then takes his turn to nibble at the corn. As soon as the corn bag is empty, the mother goose emits a low, honking sound, and immediately the six goslings fall into line again and follow the mother out into the creek to look for more food and to find a place to rest for the night.

23

Years ago farmers drove their teams of horses and wagons on to the marsh to cut the salt hay, which they stored in barns for their animals to eat during the winter. Today the salt hay is no longer cut, and most of the saltmarsh inhabitants leave the marsh, or burrow into the mud and sand during the winter months. The horseshoe crab leaves for deeper water; some of the birds fly to a warmer climate; the muskrat snuggles into his dome-shaped home.

Northeast winds drive snowflakes across the open spaces, turning the now dull brown marsh to many shades of white and gray. Chilling winds freeze the salt spray, and chunks of ice lie scattered here and there, suggesting that the marsh is a giant bowl sprinkled with huge white grains of sugar. Occasionally, a sea gull will soar overhead looking for a clam or perhaps a stray green crab. But everywhere the marsh is frozen. The tidal creek is crammed with salt ice that sparkles from the rays of the low winter sun, and the hungry sea gull tilts its wings and turns toward the sea and the beach by the shifting dunes.

Sand Dunes

In winter there is little life in the sand dunes along the beach on Cape Cod. Here, too, the animals have moved to deeper water or have burrowed in the mud and sand. The plants that had thrived there have died or are dormant, and the few birds that remain are busy hunting for food. But when the sun climbs higher in the sky, and when winds turn warm, a multitude of creatures appear on the dunes, proving that these are much more than huge piles of sand. Instead, dunes offer shelter for the common tern, a bird that builds its nest between crevices of sand. The eggs of a tern match the color of the sand, and each one is dotted with speckles, causing the eggs to look like a pile of pebbles. Because of this coloring, the eggs are protected from predators, since they appear as a natural part of the dune. So much are they a part of the dunes that they may be stepped on. But the mother tern will circle overhead if anyone comes too close, and will swoop down to frighten away strangers. Animals that hunt tern eggs, such as the visiting raccoon, learn that speckled eggs are very difficult to find.

When soft breezes dance across the dunes from Cape Cod Bay, they blow through the thick tufts of beach grass growing on the dunes. The sound the breezes make is like that of a distant train whistle blowing at a crossing. Strange circles are created in the sand by the grass as it blows back and forth, giving the impression that an unknown creature has swooped down, drawn pictures in the sand, and then swept away without leaving a footprint or a trace of its appearance. Beach grass is a very common sight on the dunes, and since it is found above the high tide along the beach, it makes a good hiding place for certain animals.

An animal with two nervous eyes peeks out from behind a clump of grass. Then a small, furry form bounds across the sand in graceful leaps. It is the long-tailed, white-footed mouse, which has white feet and legs and very large eyes. It appears mostly at night, hiding under boards or logs during the day to escape the sun. Its nest is made of bits of fur, sea-gull feathers, or dried grass. An old automobile tire, partially buried and rotting on the beach, also makes an excellent home for the mouse and its family.

Above the high-tide mark in the dry sand many peculiar-looking holes can be seen, but there is no sign of life and no telltale footprints in the sand. During the hot summer nights, a small white bug crawls out of one of these holes and hops along the sand looking for food. It is the sand hopper or sand flea, and if disturbed, it can dig its way into the sand with great enthusiasm and can kick the sand ten or twelve inches into the air. Anyone can find this little bug by cupping his hands and plowing the sand away from the hole in a circular motion. Soon the many-legged tiny animal will fall from the slope and land in the bottom of the hole.

The beach pea is one of many plants that grow on a Cape Cod sand dune. Unlike other plants that have deep roots, beach plants have wide-spreading roots that catch as much rain as possible. The cottontail rabbit waits patiently during the spring while the bright, purple flowers of the beach pea bloom. By the middle of summer, the beach pea is covered with peapods that look like miniature pods of garden peas, so the cottontail wastes no time, twitching his nose and nibbling until he has had his fill of the beach pea.

In the fall, boys and girls who live near the beach smack their lips when they think about homemade beach-plum jam from the beach plum that grows on the sand dune. The tiny, purple balls of fruit are picked and then boiled with sugar to make the delicious jam that emits the sweet smells that fill the salty air.

The Tide Pools

The marine animals that live in the bay along the Massachusetts coast under the shadow of the dunes are indeed strange. One of these animals, found in the small pools of sea water that have been captured near the rocks, fastens itself to the underneath part of a rock in this miniature ocean. It looks like a pincushion, and people sometimes call it the "porcupine of the sea." It is a sea urchin, and its many suction feet help it to creep along and to stay attached to the rock. Its underside has five hard teeth in the center which are used to scrape the little green plants, or algae, off the rocks for food.

The starfish also lives among the rocks with the sea urchin. It is slow moving and commonly has five arms, although some starfish have more than five. The suction cups on its underside, plus a sticky substance which it exudes, help it to cling to the rocks as it creeps along looking for food. At Christmas time starfish may be collected, then preserved, boiled, and dried. When these are painted gold, silver, red, green, or blue, they become special ornaments from the sea to be hung on Christmas trees. Another unusual ornament is the cast or shell of the horseshoe crab that is left on the beach after the crab molts. When sprayed or painted, it, too, makes an attractive ornament for a Christmas tree.

Attached to many rocks which are exposed above the water at low tide are small white cones the size of pearls. These cones are the homes of barnacles. At first the baby barnacles drift around in the sea and then attach themselves to a rock, a piece of driftwood, a scallop, or the shell of a living horseshoe crab. The barnacle uses the lime found in sea water to build its hard house in which it stays. It feeds by shooting out a feathery wand that directs a current of water toward its mouth, thus catching the microscopic forms of life in the water.

On the bottom of a tide pool, an object that could be a tiny tree trunk with a flowery crown bends slowly back and forth in the current. It is not really a tree trunk wearing a hat, but a small sea anemone, which has stinging tentacles that flare out in every direction to poison a tiny fish or a baby horseshoe crab which it wants for food.

A much larger and different sea animal than the anemone is the valuable lobster; valuable because it is very good to eat, there is a great demand for it, and it is difficult to catch. Lobstermen go out a few yards from the shore in small boats and pull lobster pots, or traps, that have been baited with fish heads and set on the bottom of the sea offshore.

A lobster has a pair of giant claws, and it uses one of its claws to tear the fish head apart, and the other larger claw to crush its food. Most live lobsters have a hard, dark-green outer shell, but sometimes this shell may be bright blue or calico, somewhat like the coat of a calico cat. When a lobster is cooked, it turns a crimson red. Seafood lovers consider lobster a fine dish either boiled, broiled, made into lobster salad, or into a tasty stew. There is good meat in the tail, as well as in both claws. Baby lobsters are about one inch in length, while older lobsters may weigh as much as twenty to forty pounds—an almost unbelievable weight to those of us who are accustomed to the usual one to two-pound lobster.

Beachcombing

During the spring, summer, and fall, when dark clouds push across the horizon and the winds howl from the north and the east, giant waves crash upon the beach in front of the dunes. After the storm is over, the sky turns blue and is splashed with wispy clouds. The waves have brought in many things, and this is the time to go beachcombing among the seaweed and other washed-up debris, for shells, driftwood, "mermaid's purses," and many more treasures.

A mermaid's purse is a horny case, looking somewhat like a small black leather pocketbook. On each corner of it are long horns that indicate that it is the egg case of the skate, a wide, flat fish that is related to a shark. Sometimes, if the pouch, or purse, is not empty, a baby skate may be seen inside it.

Driftwood, cast on the beach by the sea, comes in all sizes and shapes, and if it has been in the water for a long time, it will have become weathered to a beautiful gray. Some driftwood can be rubbed with wax until the full color of the gray has been brought out. Candleholders can then be purchased and screwed into the wood to make attractive candlestick holders.

The shells of clams, scallops, snails, and many other sea animals washed up on the beach can also be collected, cleaned, and used for ashtrays, or glued on carboard and labeled for private shell collections. Or they may be strung on string to make beads, or interestingly arranged on painted cardboard to form a picture of the seashore. To add brightness to the picture, beach glass, which is really small pieces of broken bottles that have been smoothed by the action of the waves, may be added.

Sometimes one can find "dollars" on the beach. These dollars are really skeletons of sand dollars, or sea urchins, washed in by the waves, and are about the size of a silver dollar. A five-pointed design is marked on the tops of sand dollars. Live sand dollars have short brown or green spines and usually live in deeper water. If beachcombers find a dead dollar and break it open carefully, they will usually find designs inside it that look like five little white doves. These are a part of the skeleton of this unusual sea animal.

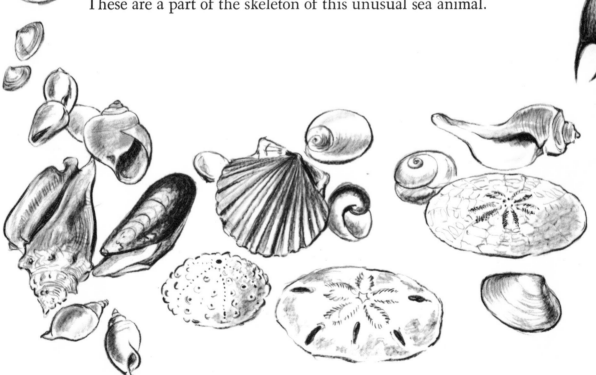

Even the seaweed found on the beach along the New England coast after a storm is interesting to look at and fun to use. Wide pieces of it, called kelp, which have long, thin stems, can be tucked inside the back of a bathing suit, thus creating an unusual-looking tail!

Common rockweed grows on the rocks near the shore, or is washed up on the beach. Each stem of this plant has a bubble filled with air, and when it is squeezed the buble will burst.

Other types of seaweed and plants called algae grow in the water on rocks near the shore in this northeastern part of the United States. Some algae are long, thin, and frail, but they are very colorful, boasting varied shades of green, brown, and red. If the algae are taken from the rock gently and placed in a large pan of sea water, they can be arranged into different patterns. Some people even press algae on absorbent paper to make decorative designs.

Small sea animals from the saltmarsh, the tidal creek, the pool, or the bay may be brought home and kept for a few days. How these specimens are to be cared for is explained in the Appendix. When the animals are no longer needed or wanted, they should be returned to the saltmarsh or to the sea. They will then slip quietly into their natural surroundings and will begin to hunt for their own food. They will be happy in the pool or in the tidal creek where the great, blue heron stands in the water waiting for a fish to swim by, while up on the marsh the black duck sits on her nest and preens her feathers with her yellow bill. Above the dune the marsh wind howls, sounding like a train whistle in the distance and blowing the beach grass in tiny circles in the sand.

Overhead the sea gull is looking for one more clam. No matter what the weather, be it stormy or sunny, warm or cold, the salt-marshes and the shifting dunes along the Massachusetts coast are interesting places to visit and to explore.

Here the bayberry with its sweet-smelling leaves tickles the nose; seaside goldenrod with its bushy yellow heads attracts the eye; and the mourning dove coos softly to caress the ear. The many plants and the animals found beside the sea will satisfy the curiosity of anyone who is lucky enough to find a spit of land that is at the same time sand, grass, mud, water, and part sea and part land, as is the spit of land along the New England coast on Cape Cod.

Appendix

Sea animals which have been collected may be kept for several days without filtering or aerating the water, provided basic instructions are followed:

1. A ten-gallon tank is a good size, although smaller or larger aquaria may be used. The smaller the tank the fewer the animals that should be kept. If a glass aquarium is not available, then plastic containers, provided these are nontoxic, may be used, such as the plastic containers for storing cookies. The tank should be washed with fresh tap water only; be sure *not* to use soap. Foreign substances usually kill most sea animals in a tank.

2. Sea animals should be collected and carried home with as little handling as possible. Some fish, for example, contract a white fungus if they are injured when they are collected, or when they are being transported. Larger animals, such as horseshoe crabs or scallops, are best carried in pails that have been partially filled with clean salt water. To prevent splashing, cover the pail with a damp towel. Small sea animals, such as sea anemones, should be carried in heavy plastic bags half filled with salt water and pieces of sea lettuce. This excellent salt-water plant, which is thin and a rich green in color, is a fine addition to a home aquarium, since it provides food for many of the animals, besides adding oxygen to the water.

3. Sea water from an area free of pollution should be used if possible. An open beach area is preferred. It may be necessary to strain the water through cheesecloth several times before putting it into the aquarium. Sand makes an excellent bottom for the home aquarium, and this, too, may be taken from the beach. It should be washed to remove any dirt or debris that may tend to cloud the aquarium.

4. A few small, flat rocks, or stones, may be used to make hiding places for animals, especially the timid ones that do not like to remain in the open. The clean sand should be spread along the bottom (about 2″ to 4″) before pouring in the sea water. A dish or a newspaper placed on the sand before pouring in the water will prevent the sand from becoming stirred. After some rocks and sea lettuce are added, animals may be put in the tank. A filled glass aquarium should never be moved, because the glass may break or a leak may be caused in it.

5. A few cups of water should be dipped out of the tank every day, and fresh sea water from the beach should be added. The fresh sea water, if poured from a height of a foot or so, will help to aerate the old water. If the sea animals do well, they may be kept in an aquarium for several weeks. Every two weeks, however, half of the water should be completely replaced.

6. Ideally, the temperature of the water should be between 60° and 65° F, and should not go much above 70° F. Ice, sealed in plastic bags, may be added to keep the temperature down on warm days. Also, the aquarium should be placed in a window with a northern exposure, away from the direct sunlight, and, as a result, the temperature will be more constant, and the growth of unwanted algae will be kept to a minimum.

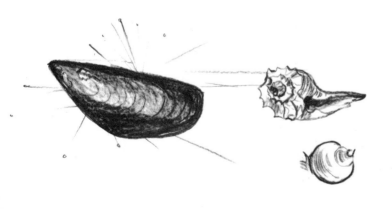

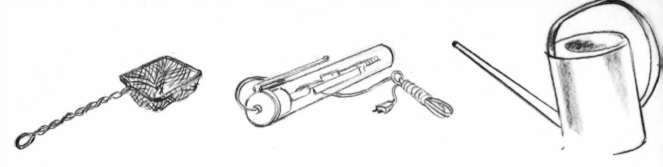

7.   Sea animals should be fed once a week. Bits of frozen shrimp or clam are best to use. Too much food spoils and clouds the water, making it unfit for the animals. Green crabs, hermit crabs, and fish will find any food dropped on the sand. Sea anemones, sand dollars, sea urchins, and starfish should have their food placed directly in contact with them. Any food that remains in the water after a few hours should be removed.

8.   Dead or dying animals must be removed immediately.

9.   A cover, usually a piece of thick glass, may be used to prevent the entrance of dust to the aquarium and also to stop evaporation. Besides, it serves to protect the animals from any accidental spraying that might be done in a room.

10.   Aquarium dealers and pet shops carry a supply of equipment, such as air pumps, filters, and hydrometers, which are needed to keep sea animals alive for many months at a time without changing the water. Since salt water does not hold so much oxygen as does fresh water, it is a more complicated project to keep a balanced salt-water aquarium for several months.

The following books may be borrowed from the library to explain how to set up a salt-water aquarium for a long period:

MELLEN, I. M. *Care of the Small Salt Water Aquarium*, N.Y. Zoological Society, New York Aquarium, Coney Island, New York.

STRAUGHAN, ROBERT P. L. *The Salt Water Aquarium in the Home*, A. S. Barnes, New York, 1963.

WATERS, BARBARA AND JOHN, *Salt Water Aquariums*, Holiday House, New York, 1967.

Index